AF221173

GALOS, Z J

THE BODY OF THE PLANE

A Flight for Love and Hope

Ballad

Impressum

Bibliographical information of the German National Library indexes this publication with the German National Bibliography. Detailed bibliographical data may be derived from the Internet website http://dnb.dnb.de

© 2022 GALOS; Z J
© 2022 ZG-ART Cover
Producer and publisher: BoD-Books on Demand, Norderstedt.
Artwork on cover and drawings by ZG'22.

ISBN: 9783755707530

MIX
Papier aus verantwortungsvollen Quellen
Paper from responsible sources
FSC® C105338
FSC
www.fsc.org

The body of the plane

THE BODY OF THE PLANE

I have seen expectation
on the faces around me
as we embark through the
lit-up sloping tunnel to the
DC9 airplane emblazoned with
the name of a Greek hero/
and some people in midst of
the crowd we have just seen
before in the last tax-free shop
that sells liquor in a preferred
two-pack-box with an advert
promising a good present
with make-believe economy.

Faces/ somber/ disillusioned,
enquiring like the businessman
detached and without illusions
like the man who sits in the
wrong seat/ investigated by
he clued-up young woman

with her Dell laptop and the
sharp wide-awake talk.
Then as the long-haired and
mustached friend sat down
next to her/ she's nervous and
seeks another seat/ put-off
by his macho vibes.
There is tension before any
take-off/ the usual shuffling of
feet, of bodies settling down
and this pushback movements
of a bald-headed silly man
in front of me/ however it's not
easy to write into my journal
if he moves back and forward
continually on this tight air ship
sailing into the winds of hope
and it may bring some comfort
to a friend, a best of many friends
now hurt by some misfortune
as darkened clouds that have
hovered for a while across her
most fragile being...
Now it's pushing through the

inky clouds towards the free
cleared-up heights of an
'Arcadian' peace of mind
but then/ will I have some
peace I never had since
a year and a half/ seeing her
the last time?

She told me of her wings
being clipped and I still
have not let go of her body
I do cling to with tenacity
her body of a goddess that
lies stretched-out above the
sheets of vanilla-clouds
in this high-altitude flight.

The airplane like the body
that is the spirit
of that trace we still feel
we still be touched by
from stone/ tree/ and the
marble-works of man
embodied in the wonders of

their creative worlds
shining from their secular
buildings and their
sculptural dedications
with the story carved into
the plinth's surround in a show,
of a traditional procession
as the decorated *cella*-wall
in this overflow from the
sculpted fields of the tympanum
that sets the artistic tone.

Under dire circumstances
without even a task light
working on my pad
I am determined to finalize
this journey's mosaic
thought-flashes of your
country
that has drawn me like a
migrating bird above
the Sacred Rock
that has never lost its
magnetic forces on either

flocks of birds or man of culture
who seek his beloved woman
in the marble's fluted trunk
that releases her slender body
in a style of a sacred ceremony
with the horses' fiery galloping
that moves the walls and
blows the roofs sky-high
catapulting its broken
image into the four corners
of this world.

This body of the plane
that flies at high speed
into a corner of the world
I wish to be
coming from the other side
the darkest on this planet
the other/ southern-most.

A well-seasoned woman
reliable/ and one/ who does
not get her knickers in a knot
a trusted Amazon

descendant from a goddess
just like Ceres/ or especially
Athena with her protective
bronzed shield/ or else
Persephone
not afraid of the cavernous
underworld.

Here, high above the clouds
I muse in isolation from any
terrestrial life
about the deeper sense of
my existence...
Perhaps I had a journey to
continue in some yo-yo-style
back and forward movements
that will fulfill the sense for
something higher
on a level of intermediate life
important for the next life:
The unknown afterlife?
We can call it many names
always the same old thing
never changes/ never fades

as we don't know for sure
we speculate and challenge
intellectually
dissipate into a matter of a
different form.
We'll never die.

My life has turned around a
pivotal incident
that was unforeseen
yet that has been carved on
some stone somewhere...
In magical Arcadia?
Somewhere there exists that
pool of knowledge that is
accessible only to a few.
I travel with positive moods
and a saddened heart
but a joyful spirit that will
meet your soul
place it upon my slightly
welted lap
and let it still thrive
bloom like a late flower

in spring/ an exotic plant
come alive
during an Indian summer
that burns like the sun on my
exposed back.
Let me still be one with
you/ you/ you
even if we do lie presently still
but might now and then meet
as we used to meet...
Lie still and enjoy the transfer
of our emotions/ our feelings
along the fully stretched-out
bodies/ in crouched-upon
seat-embraces/
the embryo-cuddles/
in tight hugs and close embraces
we still can pull together into each
other as one/ melting together
in fusion.

There! The hill of joy and
one word: *Hidoni/* as you
did open-up in me jets of

blasts and fires...
Then we extended it and
the artist's rites of love
I wrote: 'Greek Fire!'
Wow I do know!
There was exhilaration
of never-ceasing lust
indeed feats of fuck for
those days we were in
our unbridled and unfettered
ways of time to ourselves
dotting desire's I's and
crossing the tee's of a
perfectly warm and natural
sexual life/ we always have
dreamed about.

The verandah/ breath of air
that seemed always to carry
tranquility
your smile that carried me
above the clouds
your face came close and
closer yet and never stopped

loving me
lips that parted
your crimson lips that closed
tightly around my excited
red penis in a way only you
have been able to bring to the
satisfactory fulfillment of our
living fantasies/ or was it the
lust we did seek that was
hiding behind some secret
expectations/ some trust
we built and then we had
our yearnings cultivated to
this extent of physical and
mental burn I did feel with
you/ and died with you
little by little/ still...

Can you be mine with your
being and your touches
however faint, however
restricted
however we are able to love.
We love!

Tell me/ have you something
important to tell me?
A story perhaps?
An anecdote/ or introduce me
to a life you could not depict
entirely yourself?
Maybe I had to meet you
so you'll be able to.,
I will/ dedicated to you
I will!
Perhaps we can elope
for some treasured hours
be together in such ways
nobody has been together
before/ or so we'll try to
carve this unusual love into
the frieze we have to finalize
on this great temple
we have built together
as late in life/ but never ever
too late! Never!

There is the river that
flows into which we cannot

step twice
we have found that out
perhaps not the way we wished
we had to
not in a way whereby there is
more suffering of our bodies
penalized in such cruel ways
that is to me so unfair
that is to you the heaviest
burden in your life
but then after the initial
burst of tears and a deep cry
of your heart.

We have been to a new
start of a life
you have accepted face-on
with the tenacity of your will
to stay alive
while I have selfishly thought
only of physical love at first
but then the strings of my heart
were moved gently
by your voice that gave a call

to my innermost core
stirring me with compassion and
love
you had perhaps expected
and not the vibes that
rendered me suddenly ill
lying down/ falling to the ground
and offering my suffering
to the gods for some counteracts
that might help you to
understand a love that has been
transferred
from one fiery state of heart
into another dear heart
that holds now itself above
everything else.

The pain of your ordeal
sometimes runs through
me like liquid lead in my
veins and I sink tired into
my bed/ more exhausted
from the vagaries of an
unwanted separation

than from my daily chores.
Moved from your suffering
of pain I have felt in more
than one way
and I was close this morn'
of a day in May to my own
suffocation on one fair
Saturday
but got lucky with some
instant help:
Oxygen for an asthma
attack
Doc Sam told me with her
concerned mode of voice
saving my life
helping me to cut down on
constantly growing fears.

Then I knew that I will
still live
still to have a chance to fulfill
one more heartfelt wish
well/ hopefully many more/
to see you

enclose you in my arms
and then heal you.
Heal you like you did heal
me once
when I was down.
But now with the advent of
another silver-lined flight
another sailing across the
oceans of wintry skies
I seek to be close to you
in a way I have never been
close to anybody before.

Do I sense some deeper fear
than this physical discomfort
of a flight at night/ wedged into
a seat that carries the least values
on transcontinental flights?
Whatever my fears mean
there is still the fear of having
not enough strength of love
left in me to give to my beloved
not enough love to heal her.
I have to pray with my soul

and then project my total
believe into her
almost the same as the team
Pericles' did
to enthuse in each other a belief
to create the masterpiece
of all Classical art with his great
and incomparable team.
How many pieces of art may
we still write together?
How many still?

I have drawn something of
a dot and then a dash that
grew tentacles and became
almost immediately the
outline of a derriere of a
pretty woman
some other piercing of fingers
and limbs
and the music of a sonata started
to flow from my pen into
This valley and hull and the sea
with its soft-golden beaches we

lie upon/ cops of trees
we stood under
tightly embraced and with dreams
that still grow and have not
burned down to ashes yet
cinders of it still glow in our
hearts.
There is fear in all of us
sharing sides with greatness
to grow richer inside.
Let there be many days of
sunshine and more days
that enable us sailing to an
island
or to visit some sacred places
and even if all cannot be
repeat visits but to only a few
as with an inner immersion at
the temple of Apollo in Delphi
we will create our own designed
especially one
in our imaginary world.

I feel like Ulysses at times

in search of you my beloved
passing various Sirens
but such distractions are solely
itching desire's surface
and halt at the door to my soul
denied deeper access by heart
and mind
perhaps just a tinge of titillation
will do for some smiles
miles above in the skies
distract from frightful moments
take my mind off so-called
Asphyxiating allergies.
For we are just visitors on
this planet/ we come and go
continually changing our
faces
retain similarities within the clan
of the ten defined tribes
we did belong to originally.
In the middle of the night
Sleep is shallow
cannot last until early morning
now is then the time to empty

one's bladder
onto the sea of clouds
in an instant freeze –
your only chance to piss upon
the darkened lands below
collectively
in unison.

Some time's in hand and
however hard I try to find
some words I wish to send
to you/ I know you'd feel the
sense of my articulation that
flies towards you with the speed
of thought's flashing light
the future that lies behind
walls of metallic shields that
gleam like icicles and crystals
in this dawn of another given
day
whose night we have
surmounted/ scaling the
thirty thousand feet of height
that suits the burly captain's

economic fuel strategies
the laws of Newton and then
also us/ settled down at last
without the twisted tail-end
shaking
with this silver bird's flight.

The hip-jean-ed Siren moving
past the aisles with her bumps
into feet and elbows
yet this flight of new rules
and orders
this sailing that follows old
and tried-out routes
along the entire length of the
second largest river of this
globe/ called: Nile
has not yet revealed all its deeply
rooted answers
nor has it made sense to a
dropout at mid-air and join
the darkies for some tribally
rooted dance.
Gone are the days of

Solomon's mines
the fashionable adventure
that Africa did provide for
the hunter of the 'Big Five'.
And where the tent of the
protagonist had supposed to
stand in the shadow of a
wild acacia tree
the view –
once not spoilt by
any commercial undertaking
left the poet with a full view of
the Kilimanjaro and Mt. Kenya.
Old Jochen comes and thrives
with photo shoots at dusk
depicting two frozen Watussi
worriers
their sharp defined spears
pierce the night-covered
skies.

There is Aleta, in the dark
ultramarine coat that covers
her feet and highlights

her dusky-eyed appearance
in a way a plant unfolds
nourished by a waxing moon's
cool rays that lie
sensuously in the nude of
the night shadow's arms
intimately intertwined
here/ in her domain
living and loving within the
rhythm of the waxing and
waning of the moon.

Then the airship lands and
smoothly touches the Attic
grounds like a lover sinking
on top of the beloved's body.
The air is fresh still and the
swift trip to the city in the
early hours of the morn'
due east the crack of dawn
appears already and the cabman
stretches into the air and he
breathes out noisily,
pointing to the tall and dusky

pines
as if he hadn't seen a tree for
for such a long time.
The doorman's fallen asleep
the room ready
we fall immediately into the
fresh made beds.
Messages will start to fly
with the blinking of eyes
with every heartbeat I know
she'll be soon there
even if we are asleep.
In the later morning's wake
I get out and will walk as
I did many times before
my feet find familiar ways
passed the ripped-open
grounds that had revealed
for such long time its core's
intimacies to the world
it's my turn now to reveal
my heart again to the one soul
that has been one with mine.

An Indian summer

And then the moment has
arrived:
I stand in front of the man
the most friendly spouse
I ever knew.
He throws his arms around
me, kisses my cheeks
we embrace.
Then there is she/ I kiss her
cheeks and we talk and then
he will leave and I will ask her
to embrace me freely
but she aches/ still there is
a moment of intimacy/ even
if we cannot immediately act
upon our feelings to fall into
wanted bed of our desires
as we used to.
Now just a tender kiss -
followed by some more kisses
the time is beyond us with past
exhilarations and hard love
yet still present in every body's
corner and fiber. Yeah!

Still I sense her readiness
and her legs will open
when we talk and sit close
together.
Then just as if we have met
for the first time
we behave with gentle love
yet respecting the other half
as if we would be a married
couple
the hearts still telling:
We are sweet/ sweet lovers
not quite finished yet with our
love lives and we want it all
we want to live it still.

Since I kissed your lips
awakening to your tenderness
sweetness stirred up my loins
your sweetness
ever present –
my mind flies to you
since I've touched your face
felt its soft-lined shape

that I wished to kiss/ taste
absorb its smell.
And my senses fold around your
body's pelvis
I dare not to press too hard
against mine –
Almost frail our bodies touch
but waves of love vibrate
through my skin
as I kiss your lips
close-up/ closer still.
Feeling like old times.

Acropolis extreme-tourists
everywhere-Feast of ecotourism?
Wonder how many really have an
inkling of the sense of place/ and
feel the vibes of this sacred site?
Walk down through the
shadow-spreading/ scented
darkened pines
mastering the rolling pebbles below
the tired feet.
The way down from sliding to the

flattened places:
Agora of 'Attalos' and the
Byzantine church of a thousand
Years.
The air is favorable for a walk
on our first Sunday back together
in Greece.
Once again.
This time not as energetic in our
minds
but our bodies just will make
it though
B's just moving a bit better
Kores/ Archaic smiles remind
of the beautiful Indian girl
at a shop in Jozy.
Masses of people will beat all
all shards in their swelling
numbers – Sunday –We thrive
on artifacts/ the delicate carvings
of the frieze!
The grand temple.
The majestic magnetism of the
precinct

that has been walked upon since
two and a half thousand years
the rock is walked down smooth
polished by billions of boots and
shoes
rocks amalgamated from the
sacrificial blood of refuge seekers
slain down by imbeciles
as always innocent blood feeds
the ground's stampeded clays
upon which the white
crystal clear temple
finally will rise.

Then her face turns up now
pale/ soft skinned like the one
I stand before
sculpted many thousand years ago
now held in my hands and
not just sampling with my eyes
behind the clear Perspex cover
that holds it gently and I can see that
she is in a dream
a permanent detachment

from the real life that is to me
unreal
in itself an enigma
like in the Acropolis Museum
where the *Body of the Plane*
had me detached/ taken gently
and placing me upon
The Sacred Rock –
I sit and stare upon the shards
feeling myself a shard in this
planet's life
although such a great part
as I have become of her
almost as great as a son is
to a mother
a gemstone/ as lovers think
of their love as a crystallized pair
of themselves/ of their isolated
beings that have yearned and
desired
found each other and then
fulfilled the want of their
lascivious bodies
that fitted into this puzzle of

their unusual love
dove-tailed tightly and almost
completed in the intricate
pattern that fate had laid out
and opened-up in parts
that will form a whole
in this *Body of the Plane*
that has since evolved from
the dust and the stones
and flown back and forth on
days to be determined
by the cup of their desires'
overflow.
And then the pain had reached
its upper limit
when he will find the rush of
feet and the roads quite dull
and only in his heart
the flame of belonging and
love will still flare-up as
closer he will walk/ struggle
up the hill and run towards
the plane that was once such
a great a thrill and exhilarating

vibe to his being that has since
covered such great distances
such wide-open spaces
to be with her
having heard *Hiob's* message
of her battle with the man
who holds the arching scythe.
Hold-on! I cry to her, hang on!
I cannot shout, the words will
not come as usually out
but there is one pain that shoots
through my heart and drives
hot tears from the eyes
let them roll down my cheeks
and neck and heaving chest
until we catch our breath and we
then build another road
another bridge yet again.

To suffer one's death and to
be reborn is not easy.
This is the handwritten note of
Fritz Pearls/ in a book Anna gave
me to read

while we had discussed
Gestalt philosophy before
but never did I have a
chance to go into it some
more.
But now/ with love to turn
into another phase
I can see the tunnel of light
that opens up again/ but why
does it signal to me death?
A death we have to suffer to
be reborn?
Even if we suffer just the
moments
we can elope together to
the woods/ the ferns/ the firs
of a scented love-bed in a
stealthy love for now
for more/ forever more
we have a need for each
other. Yes!
More and more
and in ever-increasing waves
day by day

we patiently sit and brew
the boiling blood into a lover's
dew
we'll drink from each other
any way we muster
we have to.
Any way these days dictate
the secret cloth of environs
we escape to/ flee to
just live together like
man and woman want to live
together for a while.
Just us/ nobody else/ just us!

In the early morning hours
when dogs and cats still sleep
and only ghosts are due to
move about
I wake to the reflux of the
acidy life that has befallen
the tummy of my spouse
I sleep next to and wake as
she wakes
even as I identify with Anna

Aleta and Anetha
the three muses of love
lust and pleasure
that determine most vividly
the aspects of my words
that spin in my mind and
turn as a merry-go-round
in my heart and such is the
movement of my pen
that adds syllable for syllable
to the blank pages in my
book
I carry on me at all times
to be ready.
This Body of the Plane
has now buried itself deep
into the underground and
it travels to places
not usually visited by us
except that I go where Anna
goes
wherever Aleta will vanish to
and Anetha calls me from the
borders of her being that I am

suddenly drawn to
a part of/ identified with her
as the one I'm in love with.

This is my life now. Your face
that had been battered by the
painful pangs of suffering
has faded just a shade
but now came back to life in
a close-up reborn hug and
kiss.
A continuation of our love
that has no set rituals
but only one –
that of the hearts.
And if life is a fleeting joy
and a ray of sun caught in
the smile of plants
the vibrant red of poppies
that move their delicate skirts
in front of me
skirts you used to wear to
show-off your shapely legs
I much admire

legs I do adore and ask you
to fold around me like the
skirts of delicate poppy
leaves
I push-up like the breeze
to unfold in front of my
eyes
the pink and purple wonder
of your quim
I kiss and put my lips to
its coral arousal.
This is the life I have to
live
the life I wish to be in all
the time.
The life that lets me breathe
and shapes the movement
of my thighs on you
the shape we merge and
vacillate
the shape I feel the best in
give and take
in push and pull.
The growing desire that

builds and swills the
great and incomparable
temple
the rocky outcrop in the
midst of the city
the ups and downs of
legs and thighs
the joy and flow of a fiery
ride
almost instantly even if still
repressed and held-back
for the proper moment
that'll come now any day
for we wish to be in merging
amalgamation of all of our
beings dry or wet
intense or tender
fiery or slow I want you now
and even if I can only
manutate/ fellate and
cunnilingue
slide and fold
press and burn as fast as
our ailing bodies do allow

I wish to be with you in
any kind of fuck,
in any kind I've read about
dreamed about
and in that moment
I meet you as our bodies
will dictate and our minds
wish to merge
at that sacred moment.
Oh! How much I wish to
have a coitus mammilla
and whatever coitus we
want
then to fuck your lips so
much/ though gentle as our
excitements will grow
do take all/ absorb and
we will cope with.
Coitus! Intercourse!
Lascivious screw!
Lustful fuck with love.
In all of it: unusual love.
Stealthy love.
Hidden in the jar of erotic

dreams and lewd fantasy
we've opened-up since
we met again!

And the Body of the Plane
has landed over and over
again.
This time it is in places we
have not been to before
but we will go to now.
Perhaps it is finally
due!
This landing in a desert of
stones and melting into the
dust
to be shaped into square
blocks that are cut continually
into fitting parts of a tympanum
a column or an architrave
into some parts of marble or
stone that for generations
has been gauged-out like eyes
of the face of the temple walls
the body-shafts of columns and

the blood of the stones
generations on generations
trample upon forever
seeing the marble bodies they
do not see/ nor imagine
just be there in the dust of times
bring home a small stone
a souvenir and throw it all
overboard on their next trip
forget what it was all about.
See?
And: *The Body of the Plane*
has landed many times
brought back waves of people
and tourists/ visitors from all
places on earth
to unite at least in spirit and
good will here/ at the cradle
of Western civilization
the first place of democracy.

Today/ in the wake of wars that
rage in the world
we must be reminded of conflicts

back in antiquity
bow our heads in sorrow
for those who had lost their
lives
had no right to choose otherwise
like I think of mom/ who had
jumped from her bedroom
window
injured herself to flee from the
attack of a drunken soldier
a rape she wanted to avoid
bad times for all of us/ hers
to suffer all her life for that?
Her husband hijacked from
her life
her injury fatal to her spine.
Is this she had been punished
for?
What is life/ but an unfortunate
duck and dive?
Taking calculated chances
all the time/ purely to survive?
Now my love has reached a
bumpy road ahead/ but then

she'll survive/ she has to get
well.
Fate with its threesome cynical
laugh
an unfair advantage above
some human tragedy
some illness/ like the *jack-out
of the box*
to leave a dark and sinister
face. Not now. Not ever
we'll fight back to the end.
Happiness has not yet ended
never will...
it cannot be destroyed
by such mean bombs/ or
cowardly maiming
shots of penetrating lead
or hits that have not found
their target entirely.
Wounds that have been ripped
open
we'll bandage and plaster:
Love will always heal.
Love will always win.

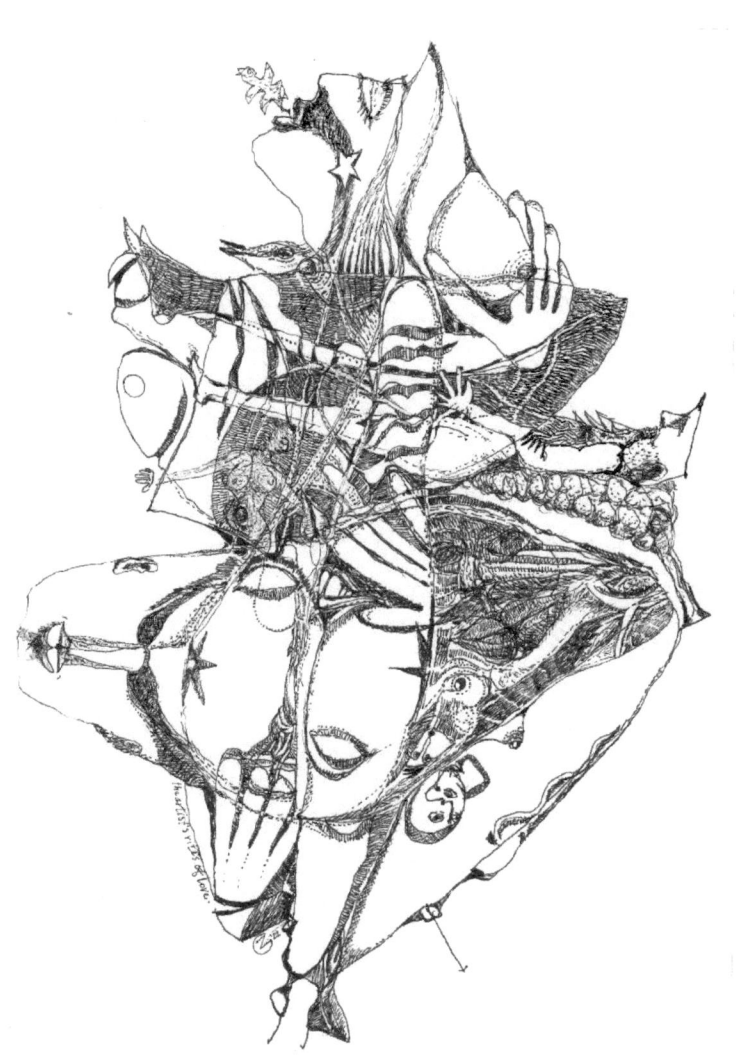

The artist's rites

I love the Acropolis of Athens
he told the man from Argentine
who is in the trade of gold.
Imagine/ he said:
Goddess Athena in her
Chryselephantine splendor
that's what is missing here –
The Holy National Treasure
he always gets upset about
the hijacked treasure
man's greedy pilferage and
war against the Nation far more
advanced than their Barbaric
own.
It is never any better/ just the
stealing will get smarter and
problems will heap-up as always
at the threshold of the protector's
door to her sanctuary
her sacred domain reduced to
carefully administered shards
that will be put together piece for
piece again.

It is only stones/ the man from
Argentine said/ people are more
important he thinks and also
the habitat's atmosphere.
But not to the poet always, who
can see the personifications
in the marble's art/ the statues
that carry their own/ inner lives
regardless what the man
in the street has to mumble
about.

Then this sleek long silver and
blue body of the plane had
landed/ *Filolaon/* a man with
one eye behind the darkened
shades of brown amber smoked
glass/ but not a Cyclops,/ kind
observant and polite
talking about the 'Story of O'
the story of some woman he
saw on the liquid crystal screen
newest and latest technology
he admires more than the

lesbian love scenes late at
night/ or early in the morn'
when he wakes-up to his
itching over-worked eyes
that hardly close/ always seek
some new images
close to his inner heart of
loving the new technocratic
aegis
wishing to absorb it entirely
into his ancient shop on the
foot of this 'Great Rock'
he calls the destiny that
did not yet fulfill man's
dreams entirely
but will in time/ he's now
convinced.
Like the poet is deeply
convinced about Aleta
who lost one arm and
Anetha/ who lost one leg
with Ana/ who succumbed
with one deep sigh and at
Eftechion

the raindrops wetted the visor
and the screen
that did lie between them
but nonetheless disappears
as a barrier/ as he still can
feel her skin/ stroke her hands
and feel his rising arousal
that flashlight-signal of his
desire's red light
that fluctuates all the time
he is close to her.

And: *The Body of the Plane*
has landed in the dusky street
of a suburb that blends the
hot and sticky air of its blasted
exhaust fumes that shape the
space of our meetings
when we eat the soup you
have cooked with the skin
of your teeth
then the fruits fell off your
body's tree
strawberry-crowned breasts

and ivory-smooth torso
shapes that carry-on the
traditional songs and this
Sabbatical dance that will
bring up the ghosts of your
ancestry/ friends and lovers
as do mine.
Perhaps they all could meet
as we meet
and tell us
about their own love affairs
their own mishaps
and console us with their
point of view.

The child of the sun that
revolves around the sacred
rock
the Propylaea greet sun drenched
behind the stage of blue
and reflect in the painted
walls.
The slim frames of windows
the blue of the Med's sea

condensed and shaping
the lines/ boundaries of views
that crystal clear depiction
postcard-view in one of the
mirrors
telling us all about
Lycobattus hill.
Green-gray lance shaped
olive leaves
transformed from the Goddess'
mighty spear's head.
Just one step separates from
the idiots the sane
the crazy wasp-nosed fellow
men
from the quiet/ tranquil
Shepherd-style of convalescence
from the edge of the bustling
restless thrill of cheap
projections of being important
hammering it into other's
limited visions/ destroying
gentle thoughts and watercolors
of one's worldly visions.

I flee quickly into the zones
restricting the festering youth
with the hammering fists of
stupefaction that satisfies
their senseless deeds they
call a life/ merely a cage of
self-destruction
winding as a python around
their cracking bones and their
diminishing lacerated heads
where it has dried-out the
bone marrow to sustain a brain
that lost all the windings
of the path of the only truth
they ever had a chance to
find.

He was searching for:
The Body of the Plane
that had given off the sound
of a jet crashing into the
historical dust of ground
the *Eridanos* that absorbed
its heavenly fall and brought

the passengers to follow the
sacred way to Elefsina/ Eleusis
a mere twenty *stadies* away
prepare the long half-day walk
but more so to enlighten those
who are selected to be
initialed into the
Elefsian Mysteries.

This indeed is a strenuous
walk in the midday sun
up the hill to reach/ like the
Panathenaean procession
firstly did at the foot of the
Acropolis.
He chooses a white and
blue-painted tavern with a
collection of old and playfully
designed frames of
mirrors/ with their gilded
decorations
against the simple elongation
of the *Stoa of Attalus*
in the nearby distance

as the start to his inner dialogue
of questions and answers.
Can he listen to the intense
complaints and the voice
thrown across the city of shards
that will either praise or condemn
his efforts to love a woman
who has been left at the wayside
to struggle with her demons
who wants to steal off her being
the best of years
of a remaining life?

He'll come to her aid and
he sends all others on the
way to the mountains and lets
them slide across the granite
rock
the slippery polished paths
while he'll attend to her
innermost needs.
He intends to love her until
she heals completely
it's his only belief right now

not the gods or the sacred
sites/ neither nymphs nor
satyrs
but the human touch of
merging senses
the ardent *Kiss of life*.

The morning's fresh air filtered
into the crevices of a night's
restless sleep with some rosy
faces to the waning moon and
a message to come
even if he could not have a dive
into the pool of ice-cream
sweetness he had dreamed of
most of the night.
Washing carefully he will now
dress and slide into his dark
and sweat-free garb most
athletes wear/ micro-woven
excellence of new-age fibers
wishing it could be his heart
he'll donate her in order to
survive the beating

penetrating hammering of the
giant city's tentacle limbs.
It is difficult to escape any of
It/ unless one climbs a hill and
then submerges into the sparse
and soft green land
below the olives and pines.
Into a door that opened and
led them into its cool and
white-blue inner life.
Ice-cream frappe and
mirrored delight.
He stares and likes reflections
that seem to close them in
from this surrounding hill
of *Pnyx*.

Then they enter this world of the
plane that folds tightly around
them in their sleep.
This morn' he shaved quite carefully
And prepared himself almost
like a lover for his first and
 most important rendezvous

yet it is perhaps
turning-out to be more for her
than for himself and he is on
his way to give her joy and some
merriment/ love/ compassion
that she'll feel as much as he
when her hands touch him
and arouse his being
wake his desires to be with her
at all times
with her/ indeed!
He has not faltered in his love
since she's fallen from the first
floor of skies
on the contrary/ he'll love her
even more than he thought
more than he ever knew or
desired in physical love
that now has been transferred
into all this compassion for her
that is now desire/ now it is a
flash-fired flame and now again
an impulsive need to
touch her

even to commute between
her drawn-out chair and the
bathroom to almost succumb
to the need of morn's rash
to manutate in front of her
mirror/ she stands naked
behind him
like the time she went down
on him and fellated him
for as long as he started to
be hard again and then pulled
him by the hand and jumped
with him into the soft covers
of the blue
that took them as a couple
who are in love:
A couple unfolding on their
Honeymoon.

And while she is asleep
he sits quite still and writes
the words down for her that'll
give the life of his inner world
away

give away his yearnings
give away his longings
the irresistible longings that
have pitched in him
so many times.
He cannot count the hours
Days/ the weeks and months
that have turned into years
many years.
The Body of the Plane has
melted down into the streets
and into the white-gray of the
sand stone slabs that pave
the new roads and pavements
along the Olympic Stadium
where people already
enthusiastically congregate and
nurture with their presence
the eternal flame.

He has seen her as a kid.
A growing young woman
and one in love and then
in deep sorrow

a beautiful flower he wished
to take away from its natural
garden.
Yet some winds of fortune
blew him about and across
the seas like a weather balloon
that has disappeared in
the mist of the rising day's
heavy perspiration
across the bay
of tranquil minds.

Love like time flies.

Has she suppressed her feelings
in the past?
the way she has done it at times
just now?
Or does she just indicate a
past affair?
Something she'd put off as just
an experience/ not having been
in love/ as she says?

Manutate for Love

Whatever her motives/ those
I do know are purely for the
sake of writing
purely for the ways of creating
the edge she can breathe and
live upon.
Right now she does not feel well
and sleeps
like a princess
but refuses to be awakened
with a kiss
as these kisses hurt and will
pierce her
but will they kill her more than
those piranhas that roam
freely in her streams of
blood?
Biting off all that enters
innocent and unprepared
and solely for an expression
of one's innermost love?
No! It is of course not legible
to me/ almost like Hindi
Korean or Chinese

meaning that I could relate
to her in more than a physical
way
but then feel barred and loved
and barred
switched on and off like
I used to be when in ardent
love
but then she never changed
and drew her inspiration from
suffering.
In a way she wished to suffer
but then self-imposed/ it could
be felt like a rush of blood from
some wine or spirit
switched-off again and then?

This nearness is good for me now
and bad for her
not the friendship/ not the
compassion.
I feel in a jam of suppressing
my sexuality towards her all
the time and convert all into

compassionate love.
It is the torture that I have to
bear as against the torture
she has to bear from her
consuming illness.
How long will this carry-on?
She calls on my feminine
nature and nurtures it:
Will I get mad in the end?
I do not want to come to her
any longer.
I want to go to a hotel
and screw my head off.
That's what I want to do.

But then: *The Body of the Plane*
descended into the blocks of
huge bricks and stone-shards
that shape it into a square box
on the chessboard pattern
of the city's famous streets
and suddenly he is abandoned
all alone emerging in the field
of science and the written

word
that has been collected since
two hundred years
but then the words stretched
back like the metallic particles
found in the veins of stone and
deep in the mountains
we have dug-out in our endless
search for the truth
we do seem to have difficulties
to find.
Perhaps we'll find traces
like the veins of gold
the tears of gods embedded in
stone.
Perhaps we find the gold inside
deeper in this mountain that is
too heavy at times to be carried
around!
I suffer/ the poet wrote on the
dark green cover of the library's
desk
that holds 24/ two times twelve
people

almost two sets of apostles of
research and study
who have enriched the world
before here
from here now it is his turn
as the war dispatched him
into the sacred hall of an illustrious
space
that his colleague of fame had
planned and built
that contains classical Philology
to find something about Simon
who is engaged into philosophical
discussions as he is now at times
with A'a/ and so was Simon and
Socrates.
Simonos and hobnails
but those shards of his thoughts and
work on shoes
he'd put to great use in:
Sokratikoi Loyoi- Socratic dialogues.
Informal classrooms descended
upon meeting A'a and young Lia
who continually engages in

lively talk.
An apartment/ a hotel room/ a bed
informal classrooms for philosophy.
Technitis-Craftsman/ expertise-
Learned young and elder
the art- *texhni*- of taking care of
one's gentle soul.
Skitotomos- shoemaker.
What was the problem of Socrates?
Was it the problem of Lia too and
perhaps it is relevant to all of us?
All/ who have been living in the safe
harbor of a profession or a trade.

Let me become a shoemaker
so I can converse with
philosophers like Socrates
Rather than converse with men
in power and perhaps with influence
their line of thinking and so -
philosophy might change the way
the world is run eventually.
Independence and freedom
of speech!

Diogenes/ Laertius refused the
invitation of Pericles to become
his court-philosopher.
Parrisia – Freedom of speech.
Man looking for the ideal position
to conduct philosophy/ art
literature/ excellence – *areti.*
Good life – *Endamoria.*
Strength of Socrates –
Sokratikis Ischus.
Letters: *Socraticorum epistulae.*
Between Antisthenes and Aristippus.
Self-sufficiency *Autarkea.*
Who was the first dog?
Socrates? [Founder of the cynic
Movement].
The Greeks named him poet
which name has/ as the most
excellent
gone through other languages.
It comes of this word: *Poiein*
which is to make wherein
(I know not whether by luck or
Wisdom)

we Englishmen have met with
the Greeks in calling him a
Maker (Sir Philip Sidney/ *An
Apology for Poetry).*
Free flowing-oscillating
"Hypersubjunctive" dreaminess-
Tibullus iners – refers to old age.

Is there a remedy for love?
A song/ a tune/ a reed-flute
and a walk along a busy
street?
Perhaps a monologue and a
burst of written creativity
I jog along the sideways and
the byways of love's stealthy
ride
that seems to slow down to
a trickle now as the head
shimmers in silver strands
and the eyes run a tear that
is stirred from my heart in
amatory monologues
oh how do I recall our once

eagerly pursued dialogues
like Daphnis slips his hand
down Chloe's dress
I do slip down your blouse
and shed your pants.

Will love end for all of
illustrious poets like the
lives of Narcissus/ Hyacinth
or Adonis?
Who can make the dead
girl come alive?
Who tells the girl who drank
a cup of poison to partake
in a dinner dance?
And the poet will consult
his learned colleague
Kleandros:
Against Eros no one found a
Pharmacon, except embrace
and sweet nuptials.
Kallidemos and Philetas.
Kleandros in prison does hear
From a traveler that Kalligone

Is dead:
There for the strangers
funeral came every herdsman
every peasant/ every man of
compassion and every
woman prone to commiserate
for him
the oak tree lamented
and the rock
and streams in deep valleys
and shady glens
even the hard race of the
rocks feel pity in this
bucolic lamentation
Kleandros recalls the
Legendary Orpheus.

The poet muses about
homoerotic desire
observing the written
ideal and experience of
reciprocated love
symmetrical and
heterosexual love

or obsessive/ unrequited
and asymmetrical
homoerotic love.

In Theocritus' poetry where
heteroerotic and also
homoerotic desires are
laid bare before our eyes
the sexual identity of
the love-object appears
incidental in fact
with a special appeal –
As it was forbidden in
Eugenianos' Christian world
even to speak.
You know what was in store
for you as having
it declared a capital crime
by Emperor Justinian's
Canonic Law.

Hermaphrodite –
Young boys serving
were erotic attractions

at a dinner party.
Lovely young Dryas
with his downy cheeks
fair complexion
golden hair tumbling
to his shoulders
otherwise noble and
lovely in appearance
but to me Dryas is lovely
only because he sits
facing such a maiden
the sacrifice is comely
virginal boys.
What is asymmetrical
love:
Between males then?
Erastes and eromenos.
Theocritus will write:
The earlier generations
was golden in matters
of love
for the beloved returned
the love even more.
This bronze generation is

not the same
for the beloved does not
wish to return the love.

Drosilla awakes from
the chaser sleep to the
sight of Charikles beside
her
both slaves/ subjected to
heteroerotic advances
from Parthian royalty.
Drosilla expresses the
desire to return
Charikles' love:
If you don't love me from
the depth of your soul
I think I have only half
the life I desire.
How is this good to
grieve the girl who loves
you?

Like a traveler out of the
burning sun into the shade

I fell into your arms
beautiful golden plane tree.
As I fled the burning heat
of despair and the heavy
weight of grief
you lie untended
a tall young tree
but now dry and dead
no longer living.
Such wrote Theocritus.

He wrote his words from books
and some scholarly research
that had been laid upon the
table and he found these
pages on this body of the city
that lay before him and there
some lady scholars whispered
excitedly some gossip
news beyond the other table
of the aisle
that lies among the vaulted
ceilings with dormer-windows
and its body-paint

with palmettes and olive leaves
in gold and greens and like
a laurel of literature's victory
above the ruins of life's
unfortunate shards
the joys of love he had
encountered here
amidst the richly endowed
Decorum of Philhellenes
and lovers of the arts
with her/ his Muse
and then true follower of
his rising thoughts about
those acts he calls ideal
and reciprocated love in its
symmetry
that rebounds from the hall
of books proportions
and its heavenly lid
that vaults above them
almost as precious as the
heavens do.
Almost in a perfect dream
a perfect balanced state

of drunkenness
of all erotic senses
symmetrical and that at
present being heterosexual
besides it comes as it is
desired/ she says to him
her personal stirrings
arouse him/ take-on the sound
of her sexual responses
he has never had and now
as its coming to a height –
he has to leave.

It breaks his heart and he
is unable to absorb anything
outside their richly endowed
togetherness that shines
like the light of those small
dark and intense sources
of glowing quartzes of
white energy that'll light up
their lives still to be lived.
But then there is a locked
door that signals the end

of another chapter –
The end of their phases
of love
they have been apportioned
allowed to tread upon a desire
a fire of rage without reason
burning sky high into their
after-summer
of an extended fuck
that is everywhere present
everywhere/ on every page
his fingers run across her body's
innumerable books
he has a hardship to keep up
to unfold and then devour
in consummate reading.

There is a smell in the air
like the burning of incense
and tire-burns
tire-burns of arriving and
leaving planes that queue
upon the licked flat lands
that have seen the masses

arriving
the poets and artists
the annual returning of true
and devoted friends
lovers
and future kings of letters
painted and sculpted pages
that rise in their renewed
adorations to the same gods
with different names and in
different interpretations
as life goes on to flow and
stream along the wide and
enormously populated
avenues.
The ways he had walked on
with her
before...
Time-in and time-out
bed-in and bed-out.
How much he desired to live
with her in the tiniest place
for some time still
that never had turned true

for him/ yet perhaps that will
come true one day.
Perhaps then the poet felt
rebuffed in his world of
genuine feelings he projected
to her and he noted then
her alienation
towards him.
Since two months/ since she
met her head-strong girlfriend
who set her onto a new track
of love and now/ here on the
Ship of Rock
with only one entrance
where she stood once
and wept.
Wept the same way she was
in his arms the second time
he saw her and loved her.

He wrote:

My dearest Arleta,
I know I do write to you

from my heart, sensing the
lack of communication,
that locks-out your voice,
leaves me in a state of wish
to hear it sweetened with love
and filling my being with the
need I have for you.
I miss all of it now and I do
perhaps not understand
entirely your pain,
your inner situation and by
nature I am an impatient
man in love.
Now, as you have
two months back told me
some facts and moods that
Influence your being in your
present life,
you have cast me aside
in front of your friends
to become non-existent.
But not the love that you
projected towards me,
no, but I assume you still

wish to keep me a secret
even in front of them –
To be the loyal friend
they demand that from
you.
Of course there are long
standing bonds
thicker than water,
thicker to the observer –
I hope than the actual bond
that exists between us –
The one I feel, the one that
for me is real, inside.
However I am now observing
not accusing, nor do I unduly
criticize,
just taking a summary, as
you did once towards me and
I have learned to do that
from you.
Besides, please do note
that I love you and probably
more than you'll ever know,
probably it is even self-effacing

to gauge its depth, width and
height, as it is rather large
and indefinably grand.
I think of it as I am sitting here,
opposite the granite head,
the bronze helmet of a
Worrier God,
the Ship of Stone that takes
one to one's world of dreams.
Of course I like it, rather love it
as it inspires me and lifts me up
like the southern breeze
the whistling ghost of poets
that talks to me in endless
verses...
Am I now in a closing position
to come here again and stay
and write and sample
the spirits of its famous
inhabitants and others
who would come and visit,
talk and moan,
love and accuse,
hate and enjoy,

the total scale of human
emotions
clamped together in one
concentrated spot
of paradise regained, lost
and re-conquered
as history goes, goes,
goes?
And now I do desire to be
close to you,
but sense that you are about
to cut me loose,
like the white cruising ship
that tugs at its anchor,
blown about by forceful
gusts
that prevail throughout
the morning,
before the stormy blasts
will settle and the calm
of the evening once again
prevails all night thereafter.
Nights,
by a full moon's glow,

ideal to make love,
love
I do have to do now to
myself, missing out, and
cheated
by the fate of distributing
misery, loneliness and
rebuffing any tenderness.
Tenderness that will be
effaced by your pain and
I could feel that
lovemaking is no pleasure
for you any more,
as you told me, I felt it,
you pulled your pussy from
my cock,
like getting rid of a glove,
suddenly...

And now my life has turned
about, as I observe the dusk
and dawn from this island,
on this barren rock,
I stare at in bewilderment

of a lost son,
an abandoned lover,
someone who takes his
feelings seriously,
even if he is married to
someone else and has
other duties to fulfill.
It is a great tragedy to
love someone as I do
and then have to take
one's feelings, pocket them
to have rebounding them
on oneself and manutate,
suffer night for night one's
own execution,
but the bullets will just miss,
that is this moment's
feeling still.

I do know that you always
felt I would exaggerate and
overflow in emotional richness,
but that is how I am and it
cannot be helped,

though at times few people
can appreciate such love that
is bottled-up in me.
And now I do know
being away from you
for so long and you
do not want to suffer in
addition
from emotional strain
that our love in tryst has
loaded us with,
if we will pursue it again
religiously.
Then, I would give you all
you'll need, all you ask for,
always Arleta,
woman of my heart...
always.
Never forget, love like this
is not usual,
casually it ne'er comes along
a leisurely stroll in the park,
or along a fine-sanded beach,
never arrives in frequent

appearances as a movie does
or as popular show.

And as the poet said:
This is the discussion that is
thirty three years old and
has erupted again —
but short-lived it was —
was it so:
That fucking was all right
as long as it was shielded
from the husband or the
wife. All right?
He cried out loud in front
of neighbor, wife and all.
As long as we enjoy pure,
sweet lust, we will lie,
forget the pretensions,
the bourgeoisie-ways of
life!
It is always the same old
story, the same old lie, and
who in the end really
cares?

Even if he sat-up all night
with a knife/ a Holy Virgin's
portrait,
to kill her, as he already
absconded his proposed
marriage,
he never did induce, but
nobody knew her mother
did confront him to his
lovemaking and also had
listened to,
tripping him up, closing
the tender trap.
Did she appeal to his world
of honor, his own mother had
set the seeds into his heart?
He was true to his deeds,
his believes.
That's how the story of his
life evolved.
Now as he sat quietly on the
narrow balcony of his hotel
he thought of Gianni Ritsos
who once lived on that giant

rock he sensed as his ship
he sailed the world.
There was enough resemblances
to fill a whole book, enough!

He is disappointed with her.
Shit! She is in no mood to be
his love now.
In no condition will he seek
new shores,
new opportunities, P.R.,
flowers,
anything he does.
"To flee desperate thoughts,
you can write the story of
her life", she says to him,
pointing to her pretty cousin,
Andromache, never,
she is not the woman enjoying sex
he enjoys. So, never?
He's dug-up a heart-shaped
black stone, washed-up on
the pebbled beach in front
of the hotel

floated for thousands of years,
turned-up here,
ground smooth and reflecting
eternity...
forever Inspiring to artist and
all folk..

I have assembled a whole
cast to play a story of love,
he thinks –
Listen Arleta, he writes:
Again, what's the matter
with you?
Am I not vivid enough, not
being too sexual?
Most women complain if
the man has no more hard
erections,
which I do have continually,
just to be despised, shit!
No? What is wrong?
You do not tell me, only
block yourself to me,
although you are aroused.

What?
Is this how you need my
love, my only hope for you
to heal?
I do never again ask. OK?
Telos.
And now I resort to some
average writing, as you do
not appreciate avant-garde
stuff, or do you?
Scheiss! I will retire to my
lovely bed and hold my
cock alone tonight.
Scheiss!
I am not glad we cannot love
any longer as we used to,
not with the same ardor or
overpowering frequency,
not with the same fervor and
want.
I miss lots of enthusiasm in
you,
am I getting on your nerves?
Have I outlived my useful

sexual life with you?
Besides I do not know how
much is a game and how
much are real feelings from
your side.
I have a gut-feel that you've
ditched me for someone
else.
However, I do not have to
cry over spilled ejaculate ,
I have to be my own man
now, no?
This is no dialogue any
longer, no swearing of
love we'll keep forever,
no deeper meaning, no
togetherness in love you
were seeking.
This is one great bluff,
one incredible act of acting,
one idiocy that is called:
'My Great Love'.
Don't you recall your words
to me ever?

They have now turned against
reality of the visual world,
against the reality of a love
that had all signs of staying
to become great and grow,
grow even to real greatness
but then you let it slip out of
your hands and let it go,
as always, always to the girls
who had power over you,
great influence and indeed
please see what has happened,
see how slaughtered all the
feelings now lie, scattered,
like a dog's carcass on the
tarmac of life's highway,
gutted from its innocent being
with one and final blow.
Telos?
Why do I learn still words
that will have had more
meanings if it would have
been in exchanges with you?

Poetry in an anthropomorphic world

Why don't you answer any
longer my questions
I write to you?
Have you read all the chapters
of my book?
Are you not interested in it
any longer?
Has a new project come-up
All of a sudden?
Hmmm?

There the poet's letter ends.
The pen slips from his hand
just the way she slips into another
life, in another place,
or is it into *The Great Void,*
the one she was always
talking about?

Fin

Further books by the author:
(Available in BoD's Bookshop)

In English:

Cantos Libidos – Love's Pure Emotion
Diary of an Aged April – A month in the life of a poet on the southern hemisphere.
Short Stories Part 3 – Perpetual Eros
Two Loves – Adventure in Eros
Short Stories Part 2 – Book III & Book IV
Short Stories Part 1 – From a Writer's Workshop Book I & Book II
The Vivenot Elegies – Along a Murmuring Brook
Educating Pizzy – The Artist Evolves
The Mill below Owl castle – Zol's Sentimental Education
Athens Elegies – A Poet's Lament
Zora's Mistake – The potential of a hidden error
Acropolis – Book I Fervour
Fighting Stance – Triangulation in Love
Spleen of Love – Zen and the Lake Moeris Adventure
The Fabricator – Life and death for a great canvas
King of Ice – A Poetic Legend.

In German:

Der Fabrizierer – Leben und Tod für ein großartiges Gemälde

Zoras Fehler – Das Potential eines versteckten Irrtums

König vom Eis – Eine Poetische Legende

*